C000303070

Together in Prayer
Intercessions based on biblical themes

Susan Sayers

This edition published in 1999 by
KEVIN MAYHEW LTD
Buxhall
Stowmarket
Suffolk IP14 3DJ

© 1999 Susan Sayers

These intercessions first appeared in
Living Stones – Complete Resource Book

The right of Susan Sayers to be identified as the author
of this work has been asserted by her in accordance
with the Copyright, Designs and Patents Act 1988.

All rights reserved. No part of this publication may be
reproduced, stored in a retrieval system, or transmitted,
in any form or by any means, electronic, mechanical,
photocopying, recording or otherwise, without the
prior written permission of the publisher.

Scripture quotations are taken from New Revised Standard
Version Bible, copyright © 1989, by the Division of
Christian Education of the National Council of the
Churches of Christ in the United States of America.

ISBN 1 84003 309 6
Catalogue No 1500241

Cover design by Jaquetta Sergeant
Edited by Peter Dainty
Typesetting by Louise Selfe
Printed and bound in Great Britain

Foreword

A praying church is a living organism, powered by the love of God, and directed by his will. The aim of those leading intercessions in public worship is to provide a suitable climate for prayer, both for the faithful core of praying members, and also for those who drift in as visitors, sometimes willingly and sometimes rather grudgingly.

Since our God is in a far better position to know the needs of each muddle of people who arrive on any particular Sunday, it is obviously sensible to prepare for leading the intercessions by praying for those who will be there, asking our God to lead us with his agenda in mind, rather than taking immediate charge ourselves. Then we have to give him a chance to answer! You may find that a quiet walk enables you to do this, or a time wandering round the empty church, or time spent on some of the mechanical jobs at home while you still your heart and resist the temptation to badger God with good ideas.

The ideas I have provided here may well spark off other thoughts of your own. Do use them however you wish – exactly as they stand, adapted to suit specific needs, or simply as a starting point. They are a resource to help you, not a cage to imprison you.

During the service be alert to what is being said and how God is moving among you, so that you can pick up on these threads, if it seems appropriate, during the intercessions. And if you have young children present, give some thought to how they can also be praying at this time. They might be following a picture prayer trail, singing a quiet worship song, drawing some situation they are praying for, or looking through the intercession pictures provided in children's communion books, such as *Jesus is Here* (Kevin Mayhew, 1993).

I have heard it said that since God can hear the prayers, it doesn't really matter if the congregation can't. I don't agree. In public worship it can be very distracting to be straining to hear, or isolating if you can hear only a vague mumble. Do take the trouble to practise speaking clearly and fairly slowly in the church, so that everyone can comfortably take in what you are saying. Bear in mind that nerves usually make us speed up somewhat, so speak extra slowly to allow for this.

Finally, don't recite what you have written, but pray it. Pray it both through the intentions and through the silences. Leading the intercessions carries a great responsibility, but it is also a great privilege.

SUSAN SAYERS

Contents

──THE LORD OUR GOD──

God Our Maker

Let us kneel before the Lord, our Maker
Psalm 95:6

Let us pray to the God who made us and sustains us.

Look with mercy on your Church,
with all our faults and failings,
missed opportunities and misunderstandings,
as we learn to be truly your body on earth.

Silence

God our maker
have mercy on us.

We lay before you the political issues,
the moral dilemmas and the dreams of peace
that concern our world,
and all who share its resources.
Where we can see no clear way forward
give us your vision and enable us
to be good stewards of all you provide.

Silence

God our maker
have mercy on us.

We ask you to take all our relationships
and drench them in your transforming love,
so that we appreciate one another more,
and value what each has to offer.

Silence

God our maker
have mercy on us.

Surround with comfort and reassurance
those who feel spiritually dried-up
or emotionally drained;
heal and mend broken bodies and broken hearts,
and provide clear pools of water for those
who are walking the valley of misery and depression.

Silence

God our maker
have mercy on us.

Gather into your kingdom
those who have run the race
and fought the good fight,
and have mercy on all who are at the point of death.

Silence

God our maker
have mercy on us.

We give you thanks and praise
for the wideness of your mercy,
and the personal attention
of your provision for us.

Merciful Father,
**accept these prayers
for the sake of your Son,
our Saviour Jesus Christ. Amen.**

God's Unseen Presence

Surely the Lord is in this place; and I did not know it.
Genesis 28:16

We have met here
in the real presence of our God.
Let us pray to him now.

Silence

Though we cannot see you:
your love surrounds us.

We bring to mind the worldwide Christian Church,
both leaders and people.
We ask for a deeper awareness
of your presence among us.

Silence

Though we cannot see you:
your love surrounds us.

We bring to mind the troubled areas of our world
where corruption, injustice and violence
ruin lives and damage self worth.
We ask for your renewing and cleansing.

Silence

Though we cannot see you:
your love surrounds us.

We call to mind those we have spent time with
during the past week;

the good and the disturbing conversations,
the joys and the aches of those we love.   Sick

Silence

Though we cannot see you:
your love surrounds us.

We bring to mind all who live away from home,
all refugees and all children in care.
We ask for the security that only you can give.

Silence

Though we cannot see you:
your love surrounds us.

We bring to mind those who have died recently
and all who grieve for them.
We ask for comfort to be given to the dying
and the assurance of your presence.

Silence

Though we cannot see you:
your love surrounds us.

We bring to mind the risks you were prepared to take
in becoming one of us out of love for us,
and we offer you our thanks and praise.

Merciful Father,
**accept these prayers
for the sake of your Son,
our Saviour Jesus Christ. Amen.**

Bread of Heaven

It is my Father who gives you the true bread from heaven.
John 6:32

We have gathered here
to meet with our God in worship.
Let us pray to him now.

Lord, awaken in us our need of you
and make us hungry and thirsty for you,
both as individuals and as the Church of God.
Let no other issues side-track us from seeking you,
and increase our love and compassion
so that we long to serve out your love
to the world around us.

Silence

Bread of heaven:
on you we feed.

Lord, allow our world to see the true value of things,
so that the worthless and dangerous is unmasked
and real needs acknowledged.
Guide our leaders in wisdom and integrity,
and enable us all to co-operate in proper care
and stewardship of the world's resources.

Silence

Bread of heaven:
on you we feed.

Lord, as we eat our food this week,
remind us of your spiritual feeding.
May the meals we prepare and eat together

be opportunities for drawing closer
to one another and to you.

Silence

Bread of heaven:
on you we feed.

Lord, we pray for all who need medical treatment
or are waiting in pain for surgery.
We pray for those who have become addicted
and long to be set free.
We pray for all whose wrong choices
have ended in heartache, disillusion and despair.

Silence

Bread of heaven:
on you we feed.

Lord, welcome into your eternity
all who have spent their lives coming to you
and now come to be with you for ever.
Have mercy on all those approaching death
who do not know you
but reject what they imagine you to be.
May they respond to the true and living God
and know your love for ever.

Silence

Bread of heaven:
on you we feed.

Lord, thank you for feeding us
with spiritual food that satisfies our souls.

Merciful Father,
accept these prayers
for the sake of your Son,
our Saviour Jesus Christ. Amen.

God Knows

O Lord, you have searched me and known me.
Psalm 139:1

Let us pray to the God who has watched our growing
throughout our lives, and loves us.

Lord, there is nothing hidden from you.
All our thoughts and plans and secret fears
are open to you, even when we try to hide them.
Deal with the doubts and misgivings
and fears of your Church,
with the love and mercy which are part of your nature.

Silence

Gracious God:
in you we can trust.

Lord, you feel for the oppressed and the forgotten;
you understand the damage which can lead to violence,
the insecurity which can lead to defensiveness,
and the neglect which can lead to lack of control.
Heal the nations; restore what has been lost;
and turn our hearts to discern your will.

Silence

Gracious God:
in you we can trust.

Lord, you see the point at which
discussions turn to arguments
and preferences to selfishness.
You know the love inside our hearts for one another
that sings and dances and aches and worries.

Work on us now in the depth of our being
and bless our loved ones with a sense of joy.

Silence

Gracious God:
in you we can trust.

Lord, you suffer with those who suffer
and weep with those who weep;
we, too, stand alongside them now
in whatever pain, distress or sorrow
is engulfing them,
longing for them to be comforted.

Silence

Gracious God:
in you we can trust.

Lord, your death and resurrection
proclaim the message of hope
amongst the tears of our grieving
for those who have died.
Welcome them into the eternal light of your kingdom.

Silence

Gracious God:
in you we can trust.

Lord, your way may be costly
but to whom else could we go?
For you alone have the words of eternal life,
and we offer you ourselves.

Merciful Father,
accept these prayers
for the sake of your Son,
our Saviour Jesus Christ. Amen.

The Listening God

If we ask anything according to his will, he hears us.
1 John 5:14

Our God is always ready to listen.
Let us pray to him now.

Father, continue to pour out your gifts on the Church,
so that many may be saved
and our faith may grow strong
and bear much fruit.

Silence

Listening God:
we put our trust in you.

Look with mercy on the conflicts of our world;
realign our values and goals
until they are in line with your will,
and our laws and expectations reflect your justice and love.

Silence

Listening God:
we put our trust in you.

Bless our homes and families
and all our neighbours and friends;
train us to listen to one another with full attention,
and recognise one another's gifts.

Silence

Listening God:
we put our trust in you.

Encourage the hesitant, curb the overpowering,
heal the sick, refresh the exhausted,
soften the hardened hearts,
open the eyes of the complacent,
and comfort all who are sad.

Silence

Listening God:
we put our trust in you.

Welcome into your eternity
all those who have died in faith;
may we in our turn share with them
the joy of living with you for ever.

Silence

Listening God:
we put our trust in you.

Thank you, Lord our God,
for the hope you have given us through Christ,
which enables us to enjoy living in eternity
even while we still journey here.

Merciful Father,
accept these prayers
for the sake of your Son,
our Saviour Jesus Christ. Amen.

REACHING FOR GOD

Thirsting for God

My soul thirsts for God, for the living God.
Psalm 42:2

Thirsty for God, let us pray to him now,
in the knowledge that he will provide for us
in the way that is best.

Father, wherever the Church is dry and parched
may the water of your Spirit well up to refresh and renew,
to bring life and strong new growth.
Lord, make us more aware of our thirst for you,
so that we come to you ready and eager
to receive your living water.

Silence

Living God:
satisfy our thirst.

Father, from the conflicting needs
and agendas of the world we cry for mercy,
for a deeper understanding of one another
and a greater desire for co-operation and peace.
We pray for sensitivity in handling delicate negotiations
and the wisdom which respects and listens.

Silence

Living God:
satisfy our thirst.

We pray that in all our relationships
you will make us effective channels
of your love and forgiveness.
Make us awash with your living water

so that our homes and places of work,
our shopping and leisure centres,
our conversations and actions,
are always in touch with the renewing power of God.

Silence

Living God:
satisfy our thirst.

We stand alongside all those who are suffering,
whether in body, mind or spirit,
and long for your healing and comfort,
your strength for perseverance
and your patience in the dark times;
we long for your living Spirit to envelop and sustain them.

Silence

Living God:
satisfy our thirst.

We pray for those who have come
to the end of earthly life; have mercy on them.
May they, placing their faith in the God of life,
share in the light and joy of heaven for ever.

Silence

Living God:
satisfy our thirst.

O God, how we need you!
We thank you for supplying us and coaxing us forward
with such tenderness and affection.

Merciful Father,
accept these prayers
for the sake of your Son,
our Saviour Jesus Christ. Amen.

Knowing God

And this is eternal life, that they may know you,
the only true God.
John 17:3

We know that God is here with us,
and hears what is in our thoughts and in our hearts.

So we pray for all who claim to be Christians
all over the world.
We ask for a real longing for God in our lives;
a longing that is not satisfied by anything else.

Silence

Holy God:
we want to know you better.

We pray for the different countries
and those with power and influence.
We pray for honesty, justice and integrity.

Silence

Holy God:
we want to know you better.

We pray for those we love
and those we find it hard to relate to.
We pray for more love and forgiveness.

Silence

Holy God:
we want to know you better.

We pray for those in pain
and those imprisoned by addiction.
We pray for healing, wholeness and freedom.

Silence

Holy God:
we want to know you better.

We pray for those who have died
and now see you face to face.
We pray for those who miss them here.

Silence

Holy God:
we want to know you better.

We thank you for showing us
what needs putting right,
and for forgiving us all that is past.

Silence

Merciful Father,
**accept these prayers
for the sake of your Son,
our Saviour Jesus Christ. Amen.**

Walking with God

. . . to walk humbly with your God.
Micah 6:8

Drawn by the Holy Spirit,
let us pray together for the Church
and for the world.

Lord God, as members of your Church
in this generation,
we ask your guidance and blessing
for all our church leaders,
and all in training for lay and ordained ministry.
As the people of God, we ask for the gifts we need
for the work you need us to do.

Silence

Let us walk with you, Lord:
every step of the way.

Lord God, this fragile, vulnerable planet
is so beautiful, and in such need of your guidance;
we pray for a deeper valuing
of our universe and of one another;
for your kingdom to come on earth as in heaven.

Silence

Let us walk with you, Lord:
every step of the way.

Lord God, may our homes be centres of love,
acceptance and welcome;
we pray that you will make your home among us
in each room and each relationship.

Silence

Let us walk with you, Lord:
every step of the way.

Lord God, we pray for all who are weighed down
with doubts, fears and misgivings;
all who are haunted by the past
or scared by the future.
We ask for them awareness of your constant presence
and courage to place their hand in yours.

Silence

Let us walk with you, Lord:
every step of the way.

Lord God, as we remember those
whose earthly life has come to an end,
we pray that they, and we in our turn,
may recognise you in heaven
and live in your light for ever.

Silence

Let us walk with you, Lord:
every step of the way.

Lord God, we give you thanks
for all the blessings you shower on us
along the way of life,
and for the painstaking guidance you provide.

Merciful Father,
**accept these prayers
for the sake of your Son,
our Saviour Jesus Christ. Amen.**

Hearing God's Answer

When they call to me, I will answer them.
Psalm 91:15

Holy God, you have called us
to meet and pray together,
and here we are.

We pray for those called
to lay and ordained ministry in your Church,
and for those at present testing their vocation.
We lay before you the work that needs doing here
and ask you to provide people to do it.

Silence

We ask in Jesus' name:
give us grace to discern your answer.

We pray for those called to serve you
in positions of authority and influence;
for all leaders to see true greatness as service
and true strength as humility.

Silence

We ask in Jesus' name:
give us grace to discern your answer.

We pray for those called to marriage,
and those called to the single life,
for parents and grandparents,
sons and daughters,
for acceptance of what we cannot change

and strength to live the Christian life
in our present situation.

Silence

We ask in Jesus' name:
give us grace to discern your answer.

We pray for those whose lives
are full of disappointment, disillusion and discontent;
for all who struggle with great perseverance
in difficult circumstances.
We pray for your strength, encouragement and direction.

Silence

We ask in Jesus' name:
give us grace to discern your answer.

We pray for those called, through death, into eternal life
and freedom from all their pain and suffering.
Receive them with mercy
and welcome them into your kingdom.

Silence

We ask in Jesus' name:
give us grace to discern your answer.

We thank you, Holy God, for your promise
that where two or three are gathered in your name
you will grant their requests.

Merciful Father,
**accept these prayers
for the sake of your Son,
our Saviour Jesus Christ. Amen.**

Take Us by the Hand

Even there your hand shall lead me.
Psalm 139:10

In our need and human weakness,
let us come to Almighty God with our prayers.

Unchanging God, change us from the heart
until the whole Church awakens to your love
that reaches out, nurtures and celebrates,
neither holding back from what is difficult,
nor rushing where angels fear to tread.
We pray for sensitivity and courage.
Silence   CARD

Lord, take us by the hand:
and lead us.

Almighty God, give us such love for the world
that we may pray with longing and desire,
'Your kingdom come.'
Give our leaders the grace to see
their work as service and their role as stewards;
and sharpen both the recognition of needs
and the commitment to just provision.
Silence   MISSION

Lord, take us by the hand:
and lead us.

Merciful God, break all habits
of destructive behaviour
in our homes and families and friendships.

Develop our ability to celebrate what is good
and face what is not with honesty.

Silence

Lord, take us by the hand:
and lead us.

Healing God, lay your hands on those who suffer,
so that they may know the support of your presence
and find wholeness and peace in your love.
We pray especially for those who are locked
into the conviction
that they are beyond your forgiveness.
May they quickly discover
the freedom of your acceptance.

Silence

Lord, take us by the hand:
and lead us.

Eternal God, in your unchanging love
receive all those who have died in faith,
that they may rejoice in you for ever.

Silence

Lord, take us by the hand:
and lead us.

Gracious God, we thank you for providing us
with a sure hope in which we can face the worst
and not be overwhelmed.

Merciful Father,
**accept these prayers
for the sake of your Son,
our Saviour Jesus Christ. Amen.**

——————— GOD'S WAY ———————

Show Us Your Ways

Make me to know your ways, O Lord; teach me your paths.
Psalm 25:4

As we gather in Christ's name,
let us bring to mind those
who particularly need our prayer support.

We remember those who teach the faith
throughout the Church and throughout the world.
Keep them close to your guiding,
and open the hearts of those they teach
to hear and receive your truth.

Silence

Show us your ways:
and help us to walk in them.

We remember those in positions
of authority and influence
in this country and in all societies,
that needs may be noticed and addressed,
good values upheld and all people respected.

Silence

Show us your ways:
and help us to walk in them.

We remember those who looked after us
when we were very young,
and those who have no one to love and care for them.
We remember all young families
and all the children in our community,

that they may be introduced to the one true God
and live their lives in his company.

Silence

Show us your ways:
and help us to walk in them.

We remember the elderly faithful
and especially those who are housebound
and can no longer join us to worship in person.
We thank you for the example of their faith
and ask you to increase our love for one another
across the age groups.

Silence

Show us your ways:
and help us to walk in them.

We remember those who have finished their lives on earth
and commit them to your everlasting care and protection.
We ask you to keep us faithful to the end of our life.

Silence

Show us your ways:
and help us to walk in them.

We remember with thankfulness
our elderly friends and relatives
and celebrate the way their lives
enrich our community.

Merciful Father,
accept these prayers
for the sake of your Son,
our Saviour Jesus Christ. Amen.

The Law of God

The law of the Lord is perfect, reviving the soul.
Psalm 19:7

In love and obedience, let us pray to our God.

Holy God, teach us to love you
with all our heart, mind, soul and strength,
and to love our neighbours as ourselves.
Thank you for the support
and love of other Christians in your church
and the richness of our varied traditions.
May we focus our attention on you with such love
that all unnecessary divisions between us crumble.

Silence

Lord, write your law in our hearts:
that we may gladly obey.

Holy God, we pray for our law makers and keepers;
may our laws work to uphold what is just and true.
We pray that we may live
in Godly peace and goodwill through choice,
rather than through fear of punishment;
through the desire to live well,
rather than avoiding detection.

Silence

Lord, write your law in our hearts:
that we may gladly obey.

Holy God, in all our day-to-day living
may we reject deceit and flattery,

so that our motives and behaviour are honest,
and our love for one another clear as the day.

Silence

Lord, write your law in our hearts:
that we may gladly obey.

Holy God, we pray for all law breakers and their families;
for those in prison
and those returning to the community.
We pray for those imprisoned by guilt or shame,
or trapped by physical frailty, illness or paralysis.
We pray for those whose lives are tragically disrupted
by war and famine, poverty and disease.

Silence

Lord, write your law in our hearts:
that we may gladly obey.

Holy God, we remember those who,
dying in faith, rejoice to see you as you are.
We thank you for their example
and commend them to your peace for ever.

Silence

Lord, write your law in our hearts:
that we may gladly obey.

Holy God, we give you thanks for the love
poured out to us each moment of each day,
and ask of you the grace to live our gratitude
and give freely of what we have freely received.

Merciful Father,
accept these prayers
for the sake of your Son,
our Saviour Jesus Christ. Amen.

God's Kingdom

Your kingdom come. Your will be done,
on earth as it is in heaven.
Matthew 6:10

As God has taught us, let us pray
for the coming of the kingdom in every situation.

We long for the Church to be pure and holy,
alight with God's love and compassion,
and free from behaviour which is unworthy
of God's chosen people.

Silence

God our Father:
let your kingdom come.

We long for the nations to be wisely governed,
with just laws and a sense of vision
which reflects the best of human nature.
We long for peace and mutual respect
in each community throughout the world.

Silence

God our Father:
let your kingdom come.

We long for our homes to be filled with God's love,
so we are happy to put ourselves out for others,
to listen with full attention, and to value one another.
We long to clear away anything in our life-style
which competes with God for our commitment.

Silence

God our Father:
let your kingdom come.

We long for those who feel neglected
or rejected by society
to know God's love and acceptance of them.
We long for all those in pain and distress
to be comforted and relieved.

Silence

God our Father:
let your kingdom come.

We long for the dying to recognise
their need of God and his power to save;
for those who have died to be judged with mercy
and rest in God's peace.

Silence

God our Father:
let your kingdom come.

We give you thanks, Lord God,
for your teaching and your example
which opens our eyes to your truth.

Merciful Father,
**accept these prayers
for the sake of your Son,
our Saviour Jesus Christ. Amen.**

The Seed of God's Word

The seed is the word of God.
Luke 8:11

Gathered together as the people of God,
and attentive to his will, let us pray.

Heavenly Father, may your words of truth
take root in our hearts and grow to rich maturity.
May we hear your will for us and act upon it;
may we take seriously our responsibility
to encourage and nurture one another in faith
at every age and every stage.

Silence Lord, sow your seed in our hearts:
your word is life and strength.

Heavenly Father, may every act of selfless giving
and every search for truth be richly blessed and rewarded;
Disturb assumptions and lead
many to ponder more deeply
the spiritual dimension of their lives.
May the word of God reach all who are ready to receive it,
and let us set no boundaries here as to who they might be.

Silence Lord, sow your seed in our hearts:
your word is life and strength.

Heavenly Father, make our homes
places of love and growth,
welcoming to all who visit them,
and accepting and forgiving to all who are nurtured there.
Help us through the quarrels and heartaches
and remind us to honour one another
as your cherished ones.

Silence   Lord, sow your seed in our hearts:
                           your word is life and strength.

Heavenly Father, may all whose bodies,
souls or minds are aching
know the comforting and strengthening power
of your companionship, and the healing work of your love.
May we be more ready
to support and befriend one another
through the difficult times,
in the name and love of the God we worship.

Silence   Lord, sow your seed in our hearts:
                           your word is life and strength.

Heavenly Father, we pray for all
who are making the journey through physical death,
as they put down earthly things
and wake to your presence.
Bring us all to share with them
your life in all its fullness.

Silence   Lord, sow your seed in our hearts:
                           your word is life and strength.

Heavenly Father, the rain and sunshine,
the growing and harvesting,   .
sing to us of your faithful love,
and we offer you our thankful praise
for all your gifts to us.

Merciful Father,
**accept these prayers
for the sake of your Son,
our Saviour Jesus Christ. Amen.**

Open Our Eyes

Lord, let our eyes be opened.
Matthew 20:33

In the knowledge that God is here present with us,
let us pray.

Father, we thank you for the gifts of sight and insight,
and ask you to be there in all our looking.
Help us always to see with eyes of faith, love and honesty.

Silence

Open our eyes:
to see things your way, Lord.

We pray for our church leaders
in their demanding ministry of love,
that they may be given all the support,
grace and anointing they need.

Silence

Open our eyes:
to see things your way, Lord.

We pray for the gifts of discernment and integrity
among all those who govern, advise and lead.
Clear away all self-centred ambition
to free our leaders to serve.

Silence

Open our eyes:
to see things your way, Lord.

Whenever we have eye contact with family, friends,
neighbours or colleagues,
be there in that communication,
and remind us of our calling to love one another.

Silence

Open our eyes:
to see things your way, Lord.

We call to mind those whose eyes are wet with tears
or tense with pain.
Help them to sense your reassuring love
which can bring us through the darkest of valleys.

Silence

Open our eyes:
to see things your way, Lord.

Jesus is the firstfruit
of the new and eternal life we are promised in you.
We commend to your love
those who have recently walked through death
into that promise, and thank you for the privilege
of knowing them here on earth.

Silence

Open our eyes:
to see things your way, Lord.

Father we thank you for loving us
right through death into new life,
and we rejoice in your victory over evil.

Merciful Father,
**accept these prayers
for the sake of your Son,
our Saviour Jesus Christ. Amen.**

—————— JESUS ——————

Incarnate God

And the Word became flesh and lived among us.
John 1:14

Incarnate God:
we love you and we need you.

We have been called
to pray for one another in God's presence.
Let us settle ourselves to do that now.

We pray for all who are called to lead and teach
so that the truth of God's love
is shared throughout the world.
We ask for wisdom, energy
and sensitivity to God's prompting.

Silence

Incarnate God:
we love you and we need you.

We pray for all with power
and influence in our world.
We ask for a widespread desire
for those qualities of compassion and integrity.

Silence

Incarnate God:
we love you and we need you.

We pray for all parents and their children,
especially where there are conflicts,
anxious moments and gaps in communication.

Silence

Incarnate God:
we love you and we need you.

We pray for all missing persons and their families,
all who are rethinking their direction,
all who find life full of contradictions
at the moment.

Silence

Incarnate God:
we love you and we need you.

We pray for those who have come to the end
of their earthly life,
especially any who are unprepared.

Silence

Incarnate God:
we love you and we need you.

We give thanks and praise
for God's involvement in our lives.

Merciful Father,
**accept these prayers
for the sake of your Son,
our Saviour Jesus Christ. Amen.**

The Good Shepherd

I am the good shepherd.
John 10:11

The Lord is our shepherd,
and we are the sheep of his pasture.
Let us bring to him our cares and concerns
for the Church and for the world.

Good Shepherd of the sheep, we pray for the Church;
for all congregations, for pastors
and all who minister in word and sacrament.
We pray for clear guidance and direction
in those issues which disturb us,
asking not that you lead us the easy way
but the way that is right and good.

Silence   The Lord is my shepherd:
                             there is nothing I shall want.

Good Shepherd of the sheep,
we pray for the world we inhabit –
the world we have inherited
and will pass on to successive generations.
Teach us to look after it carefully and wisely,
to share its gifts more fairly,
and work together to ease its sufferings.
Turn the hearts of those who are excited by evil things
and encourage the timid to speak out
for what is wholesome and good.

Silence   The Lord is my shepherd:
                             there is nothing I shall want.

Good Shepherd of the sheep, we pray for our
places of work, our colleagues, friends and neighbours,

and the members of our families.
We ask not for popularity at all costs,
but the grace to do your will and be your witnesses
to what it means to live lovingly,
both when this is easy and also when it hurts.

Silence   The Lord is my shepherd:
                                          there is nothing I shall want.

Good Shepherd of the sheep,
we pray for the weak and vulnerable,
for those who must live
depending on others for every need,
and for those who are bullied, or constantly despised.
We pray for a greater reverence, one for another,
for a greater willingness
to uphold and encourage one another;
we pray for healing and wholeness.

Silence   The Lord is my shepherd:
                                          there is nothing I shall want.

Good Shepherd of the sheep,
we pray for those who have died;
we pray for those who ache with sorrow at their going;
we commend them all into your unfailing care
which lasts throughout this life and on into eternity.

Silence   The Lord is my shepherd:
                                          there is nothing I shall want.

Good Shepherd of the sheep, we give you thanks
that in you we are able to live through good and ill
with abundance of life.

Merciful Father,
accept these prayers
for the sake of your Son,
our Saviour Jesus Christ. Amen.

The Way of Life

I am the way, and the truth, and the life.
John 14:6

Gathered together in one spirit, let us pray to our God.

Father, wherever our attention
has wandered from your calling,
wherever we have fallen short of your will for us,
and failed to keep the spirit of your law of love,
forgive us and transform us,
so that we walk again the path that leads to life.

Silence

Show us the way of life:
and help us to walk in it.

Wherever the Church is asked
to give leadership on sensitive issues;
whenever the current world expectations of behaviour
need to be challenged in the light of God's love,
give us the wisdom and guidance we need.

Silence

Show us the way of life:
and help us to walk in it.

Wherever our homes are lacking
in love and mutual respect,
wherever destructive relationships
cause distress and heartache,
and wherever people are made to feel they don't matter,
give a new realisation of your ways
and your hopes for us, so that your kingdom may come
and your will be done.

Silence

Show us the way of life:
and help us to walk in it.

Wherever there is illness, unhappiness, injustice or fear;
wherever people feel frustrated, imprisoned or trapped;
give us a greater sense of loving community,
a heart to put right whatever we can,
and the willingness to stand
alongside one another in our sorrows.

Silence

Show us the way of life:
and help us to walk in it.

Wherever earthly lives have come to an end,
and people are grieving the loss of their loved ones,
fill these places with the eternal peace of your presence
and prepare us all through our lives on this earth
for everlasting life with you in heaven.

Silence

Show us the way of life:
and help us to walk in it.

Father, we thank you
for the personal and affectionate way you care for us
and provide for all our needs;
may we spread the good news of your love
by the way we respond to you and to one another.

Merciful Father,
accept these prayers
for the sake of your Son,
our Saviour Jesus Christ. Amen.

We Look to the Cross

While we were still sinners Christ died for us.
Romans 5:8

As followers of Jesus Christ,
let us pray to our loving Father in heaven.

Father, help us all in your Church
to understand what it really means to love and serve you.
At the times of testing, strengthen us,
at unexpected or undeserved suffering, support us,
at the end of our energy, revive us
and teach us through it all the inexplicable peace and joy
that comes from doing your will.

Silence

We look to the cross:
and see your love for us.

Father, have mercy on us for the misdirected use
of time, money and resources in this world.
In the struggle against evil and sin, empower us,
so that justice and righteousness are established,
upheld and celebrated,
as hearts rejoice in the freedom of all that is good.

Silence

We look to the cross:
and see your love for us.

Father, renew our commitment to your loving
in all our relationships, our work and our prayer.
In the hard choices, give us wisdom,
in the painful decisions, affirm us,

and may our words speak your truth,
whether that is to encourage,
to comfort or to challenge.

Silence

We look to the cross:
and see your love for us.

Father, bring healing and wholeness
to those who suffer, in body, mind or spirit.
In the sleepless nights and endless days of pain,
give the grace to persevere with patience,
and turn these dark times
into places of spiritual growth.

Silence

We look to the cross:
and see your love for us.

Father, may those who have died
rest in the eternal peace of your presence,
their burdens laid down and their suffering ended.

Silence

We look to the cross:
and see your love for us.

Father, the full extent of your love for us
is so much greater than we can ever imagine,
and in our love and thankfulness
we offer the praise of our lives.

Merciful Father,
accept these prayers
for the sake of your Son,
our Saviour Jesus Christ. Amen.

Lord of Life

Whoever has the Son has life.
1 John 5:12

As we gather in the company of the living God,
let us pray.

Lord of life, we pray that the Church
may be alive with your risen life,
refreshed and revived by the breath of your Spirit,
purified and refined like gold and silver,
so that we truly offer the possibility
of saving love to the searching world.

Silence

You are the one true God:
and we worship you.

Lord of life, we pray that in all meetings and conferences
where important decisions are taken,
hearts may be turned to honour what is just and true,
compassionate and constructive.
We pray that in all areas
where there is corruption, deceit or distrust,
consciences may be sensitised afresh
to know what is right and strive towards it.

Silence

You are the one true God:
and we worship you.

Lord of life, we pray for the streets
and places of work we represent.
May they be places where the truth of your being

is proclaimed daily by the way we live
and handle the everyday situations, through your leading.
May our words and actions speak of your faithful love,
your graciousness and your purity.

Silence

You are the one true God:
and we worship you.

Lord of life, we lay before you now
those who are struggling with pain and anguish,
or wrestling with tragedy and conflict.
We stand beside them in their suffering
and offer it to your healing love.

Silence

You are the one true God:
and we worship you.

Lord of life, we pray for those who have died
and now see you as you really are.
We ask for mercy and forgiveness,
and commend them to your keeping for ever.

Silence

You are the one true God:
and we worship you.

Lord of life, your love for us is so great
and our love for you so small.
Thank you for accepting what we are able to offer;
and ignite us to a blaze of love.

Merciful Father,
accept these prayers
for the sake of your Son,
our Saviour Jesus Christ. Amen.

——THE PEOPLE OF GOD——

The Family of God

All who are led by the Spirit of God are children of God.
Romans 8:14

As children together in the family of God,
let us pray now to our Father in heaven.

Lord, we pray that as Christians
we may listen more attentively
and with greater urgency than ever before
to the words of Jesus;
give us more awareness of your presence with us,
both in our worship and in our daily ministry,
giving us the courage to live out your truth with joy.

Silence

Heavenly Father:
hear your children's prayer.

We pray for those who do not know you
or dismiss you as irrelevant to their lives;
we pray for those who influence and encourage others
in what is evil, destructive or depraved,
and ask for your protection
of all who are vulnerable and in danger.

Silence

Heavenly Father:
hear your children's prayer.

We pray for all who are adjusting
to new relationships in the family,
new homes or new work and leisure patterns;
we pray for stronger root growth in you,
so that we are not thrown

by the changes and troubles of everyday life,
knowing the reality of your faithfulness.

Silence

Heavenly Father:
hear your children's prayer.

We pray for all who are too exhausted
or overwhelmed by circumstances and pressures
to be able to pray;
surround all those who are troubled
and heavily laden
with the revitalising assurance of your presence,
your understanding and your love.

Silence

Heavenly Father:
hear your children's prayer.

We pray that those who have gone through death
may know the brightness of everlasting life
in your company;
may we, with them, come to experience
the glory and joy of heaven.

Silence

Heavenly Father:
hear your children's prayer.

Father, we thank you for the glimpses of glory
you give us in this life, for your friendship
and your promise to be with us always.

Merciful Father,
**accept these prayers
for the sake of your Son,
our Saviour Jesus Christ. Amen.**

Bind Us Together

*Clothe yourselves with love, which binds
everything together in perfect harmony.*
Colossians 3:14

Our God is always ready to hear our prayers.
Let us be still, and pray to him now.

Heavenly Father,
we thank you for all those who remind us
to be kind and loving by their words and example.
We pray that as a church
we may break through the barriers which separate us,
and put right whatever blocks us from your love.

Silence

Bind us together, Lord:
we know our need of you.

We pray that the lines of communication
between people and nations
may be kept open, respected and honoured,
and that where communication has broken down
there may be a new desire for reconciliation.

Silence

Bind us together, Lord:
we know our need of you.

Heavenly Father,
we pray for all those making and repairing roads,
travelling on them and stuck in traffic jams;
we pray for the towns and villages linked by roads,
for a public transport system that protects the environment,
and serves the community.

Silence

Bind us together, Lord:
we know our need of you.

We pray for those we see and talk to
every day or every week;
for those we often argue with or misunderstand;
for those who brighten our lives and make us smile;
for a greater thankfulness and appreciation
of those we usually take for granted.

Silence

Bind us together, Lord:
we know our need of you.

We pray for those we have hurt or upset;
for those who feel isolated and alone;
for the ill, the frail, the stressed and the bitter.

Silence

Bind us together, Lord:
we know our need of you.

We pray for the dying
and those who have died to this earthly life.
May they know the eternal peace of your heaven,
and may those who miss them be comforted.

Silence

Bind us together, Lord:
we know our need of you.

Heavenly Father, we thank you for helping us
to get ourselves ready to receive you.

Merciful Father,
**accept these prayers
for the sake of your Son,
our Saviour Jesus Christ. Amen.**

Hear Our Prayer

Let your requests be made known to God.
Philippians 4:6

All our needs are God's concerns.
Let us pray to him now.

Father, make us a listening Church,
welcoming to the hesitant,
encouraging to the young,
sensitive to the differences and attentive to the needs.

Silence

God, in mercy:
hear us as we pray.

Father, make us a caring world,
wise in government,
honest in promises,
far-sighted in the management of resources,
and open-hearted in charitable giving.

Silence

God, in mercy:
hear us as we pray.

Father, make us a responsible community,
supporting our neighbours and friends,
sharing one another's sorrows and joys,
and opening our homes to your indwelling.

Silence

God, in mercy:
hear us as we pray.

Father, as we remember those
who have asked for our prayers,
take their needs and provide for them,
take their wounds and heal them,
take their suffering and comfort them.

Silence

God, in mercy:
hear us as we pray.

Father, as we call to mind those who have died,
may they know the welcoming of your love
into eternal joy.

Silence

God, in mercy:
hear us as we pray.

Thank you, Holy God,
for knowing our needs
even before we become aware of them ourselves.

Merciful Father,
accept these prayers
for the sake of your Son,
our Saviour Jesus Christ. Amen.

The Breaking of Bread

. . . made known to them in the breaking of the bread.
Luke 24:35

As we gather to hear the word of God
and to break bread in the presence of Jesus,
let us pray.

Walk with us, Lord, on our journey of faith,
both as individuals and as the Church of God;
open up to us the truths you long for us to understand,
and inspire all who teach and interpret the scriptures.
Equip us all to pass on the good news of Jesus.

Silence

Make yourself known to us, Lord:
in the breaking of bread.

Walk with us, Lord, down the streets
of our cities, towns and villages,
drive with us down the motorways
and fly with us down the air corridors.
Meet all those who are curious, searching,
or moving in the wrong direction.
Let your presence be sought
and recognised in all the world.

Silence

Make yourself known to us, Lord:
in the breaking of bread.

Walk with us, Lord, in our life journeys,
guiding, teaching and correcting us,
as we learn the lessons of loving
in our homes, our work and our communities.

Silence

Make yourself known to us, Lord:
in the breaking of bread.

Walk with us, Lord,
through the times of suffering and pain,
alerting us to one another's needs
and providing for us in whatever ways are best for us.
Help us to trust you through the dark times;
breathe new life and hope
into those who are close to despair.

Silence

Make yourself known to us, Lord:
in the breaking of bread.

Walk with us, Lord, through the valley of death;
may our love and prayers support those
who walk that journey today.
Draw close to them and welcome them
into the joy of heaven.

Silence

Make yourself known to us, Lord:
in the breaking of bread.

Lord, we thank you for walking with us
wherever we travel,
We thank you that you are indeed
real and alive every step of the way!

Merciful Father,
**accept these prayers
for the sake of your Son,
our Saviour Jesus Christ. Amen.**

Love One Another

This is my commandment, that you love
one another as I have loved you.
John 15:12

God remembers our frailty;
let us pray to him now.

When conflicts threaten to disrupt our fellowship
in the church community,
deal with our frustrations and anger,
and give us the grace to forgive.

Silence

May we love one another:
as you have loved us.

When the luggage we carry from the past
interferes with our capacity to cope with the present,
heal the damage from our memories
and transform our experiences for good.

Silence

May we love one another:
as you have loved us.

When the differences in cultures
block our understanding of one another
and obstruct the peace process,
broaden our vision to discern the common ground.

Silence

May we love one another:
as you have loved us.

When the layers of resentment
have turned into rock,
dissolve them with the rain of your loving mercy.

Silence

May we love one another:
as you have loved us.

As those we have known and loved
pass through the gate of death,
have mercy on them,
and receive them into the joy
of your eternal kingdom.

Silence

May we love one another:
as you have loved us.

As we acknowledge the beauty
of loving even our enemies,
we thank you for the extraordinary love
you show us in Jesus.

Merciful Father,
**accept these prayers
for the sake of your Son,
our Saviour Jesus Christ. Amen.**

THE CHRISTIAN LIFE

Forgiveness

Just as the Lord has forgiven you, so you also must forgive.
Colossians 3:13

In the knowledge of all God has done for us,
let us bring to him our concerns
for the Church and for the world.

Thank you, Father, for the love
which forgives again and again,
and is prepared to trust us
with the care of your people
even after we have let you down many times.
Teach us to minister to one another's needs
with compassion, sensitivity and discipline,
so that all are affirmed and encouraged.

Silence

The Lord is full of compassion:
his love lasts for ever.

Thank you, Father, for the order and variety,
simplicity and complexity of this universe.
Thank you for all that humankind is able to do;
may all these gifts be used wisely and well,
for the good of all, including those as yet unborn.

Silence

The Lord is full of compassion:
his love lasts for ever.

Thank you, Father, for what we have been forgiven
and for the opportunities we have each day
to learn the joy of forgiving others.

Smash through our self-righteousness
and keep us learning in humility at your feet.

Silence

The Lord is full of compassion:
his love lasts for ever.

Thank you, Father, for all those who care for the sick,
the unstable, the ungrateful and the difficult.
We pray for all who are on the receiving end
of hate, deceit, suspicion or abuse,
and for those who cause others pain
and distress of any kind.
We pray for your healing and transforming.

Silence

The Lord is full of compassion:
his love lasts for ever.

Thank you, Father, for those whose living and dying
has taught us much about love.
Freed from their pain and restrictions of age or injury,
may they enjoy for ever the life of heaven.

Silence

The Lord is full of compassion:
his love lasts for ever.

Thank you, Father, for disturbing our complacency
and challenging us to move forward with you,
assured of your company and your love.

Merciful Father,
**accept these prayers
for the sake of your Son,
our Saviour Jesus Christ. Amen.**

Awake and Shining

Sleeper, awake! Rise from the dead,
and Christ will shine on you.
Ephesians 5:14

In the power of the Spirit,
let us pray to the Lord.

Heavenly Father, anoint your Church all over the world
with the oil of your Spirit, so that we burn brightly,
lighting the dark world with your love and truth.
Keep our church communities from error and sin,
and supply us all, through word and sacrament,
with all our souls require.

Silence   Waken us, Lord:
to shine with your love.

Heavenly Father, take the false values of our world
and upend them;
take the oppressed and free them;
take the leaders and inspire them;
take the past and redeem it, the present and fill it,
the future and guide us in it.

Silence   Waken us, Lord:
to shine with your love.

Heavenly Father, it is in our homes and daily tasks
that you train us in loving obedience.
We pray for those who have to live and work with us
and are familiar with our habits, gifts and faults.
May we make the most of the opportunities
to love, to forgive, to stand back and to reach out.

Silence Waken us, Lord:
to shine with your love.

Heavenly Father, as we pray for all who are ill
in body, mind or spirit,
surround them with your love and healing,
your reassurance and peace.
We pray for those
who are too weak or exhausted to pray,
but simply know they ache for your comfort.

Silence Waken us, Lord:
to shine with your love.

Heavenly Father, as real and living for the dead
as for those of us walking through time,
we commend to your mercy and love
those who have died in your faith and friendship;
may we all share in the joy
of Christ's coming in glory.

Silence Waken us, Lord:
to shine with your love.

Heavenly Father, all the resources for holiness
you lovingly provide,
and we thank you
for your ongoing and unlimited provision.

Merciful Father,
accept these prayers
for the sake of your Son,
our Saviour Jesus Christ. Amen.

Serving and Caring

Bear one another's burdens.
Galatians 6:2

Gathered as the Church of God,
members of the Body of Christ,
let us pray together.

Fill your Church, O Lord,
with life and energy, spiritual health and vitality.
As we feed on you, may we grow more like you;
may we exercise your loving,
minister with your tenderness,
serve with your humility and co-operate with your vision.

Silence

O Lord of infinite love:
help us to serve and care.

Fill your world, O Lord, with wonder at creation,
recognition of our mutual human responsibility,
desire for reforming what is at fault,
and hope in the possibilities of living at peace
with God and with one another.

Silence

O Lord of infinite love:
help us to serve and care.

Fill our homes and neighbourhoods, O Lord,
with the generosity and trust that allows space
but is always ready to encourage and support.
May we cherish our bodies, minds and spirits

as temples containing your Spirit,
and honour one another as people of your making.

Silence

O Lord of infinite love:
help us to serve and care.

We pray for all who are ill at home or in hospital,
for all in emergency surgery or in casualty;
for those who have just discovered
that they have injuries or illnesses
that will change their lives.
We pray for the work of all who heal and comfort,
all who visit the sick and counsel the distressed.

Silence

O Lord of infinite love:
help us to serve and care.

We pray for the dying and those who love them;
we pray for those who have completed this life
and have made the journey through death.
We pray for the work of those who comfort the bereaved.

Silence

O Lord of infinite love:
help us to serve and care.

Fill our hearts, O Lord, with thankfulness and praise
as we recall your faithfulness and live in your love.

Merciful Father,
**accept these prayers
for the sake of your Son,
our Saviour Jesus Christ. Amen.**

Heal Us and Use Us

He touched her hand, and the fever left her,
and she got up and began to serve him.
Matthew 8:15

Let us focus our bodies, minds, hearts and wills
as we pray to the God of all creation.

Holy God, you are the focus of our love and worship,
because you alone are the Lord
who has made us and rescued us.
May we not return to the slavery of sin
but live in your freedom, serving you with joy,
in thankfulness for all you have done for us.

Silence

Heal us, Lord:
and use us to your glory.

Holy God, though the world may often reject you,
you never fail to believe in us all
and love us with tenderness.
We pray for all areas of conflict, deceit,
mismanagement and greed,
and for all who are drawn into the chaos of evil.

Silence

Heal us, Lord:
and use us to your glory.

Holy God, our daily lives provide such rich ground
for acts of loving kindness,
self-discipline and courage.

Remind us of the opportunities,
and strengthen us to use them.

Silence

Heal us, Lord:
and use us to your glory.

Holy God, we thank you for all
who lovingly look after those in nursing homes,
hospitals, nurseries and prisons,
and we pray for all who need such care
and rely on others' help.

Silence

Heal us, Lord:
and use us to your glory.

Holy God, we call to mind
those who have recently died
and thank you for each act of goodness in their lives.
Have mercy on them and forgive their failings,
so that they may share the joy of heaven for ever.

Silence

Heal us, Lord:
and use us to your glory.

Holy God, we thank you
for our human potential for good,
and for your gift of grace
that makes such goodness a real possibility.

Merciful Father,
accept these prayers
for the sake of your Son,
our Saviour Jesus Christ. Amen.

Faithful to the End

The one who endures to the end will be saved.
Matthew 24:13

The Lord is always ready to listen;
let us pray to him now.

Lord, we pray particularly for those
whose faith is being battered
and those who no longer pray;
we pray for our training programmes
and our weekly worship;
for our faith to be deepened and strengthened.

Silence

Keep us faithful:
firm to the end.

We pray for those whose responsibility it is
to manage the world's economy,
and for those who have difficult
ethical decisions to make;
we pray for wisdom and courage to do what is right.

Silence

Keep us faithful:
firm to the end.

We pray for the world our children will inherit
and ask your blessing on all parents
and the responsibilities they face;
we ask for understanding, maturity,
and the gift of laughter.

Silence

Keep us faithful:
firm to the end.

We pray for the victims of disasters,
famines, earthquakes and plagues;
for all who are crying
and those who have no tears left.
We pray for comfort, renewed strength,
and available friends.

Silence

Keep us faithful:
firm to the end.

We pray for those who are nearing death
and those who have died;
especially we pray for those
who have died suddenly and unprepared.
We pray for mercy and forgiveness.

Silence

Keep us faithful:
firm to the end.

We give you thanks, Lord God,
that you always provide the grace we need
to accomplish what you ask of us.

Merciful Father,
**accept these prayers
for the sake of your Son,
our Saviour Jesus Christ. Amen.**

SPECIAL DAYS

Christmas Day

And the Word became flesh and lived among us.
John 1:14

As we celebrate the birth of Jesus, the Word of God,
let us pray with thankful hearts.

The bells and lights and presents and decorations
in church and in our homes
express our thanks to you, Lord,
for coming into the world in person.

Silence

On this Christmas Day we want to say:
Thank you, holy Father!

The world Jesus was born into was the world we know.
Thank you for being prepared to face the dangers and risks
of human mistakes and sin in order to save us.

Silence

On this Christmas Day we want to say:
Thank you, holy Father!

Many of us will be celebrating
with our families and friends.
We invite you to join us in all the festivities,
and ask you to teach us true loving.

Silence

On this Christmas Day we want to say:
Thank you, holy Father!

We remember those who find Christmas
a sad or lonely season;
we remember those for whom it brings to the surface
memories, anxieties or sorrows.
Through good and difficult times
you are always with us.

Silence

On this Christmas Day we want to say:
Thank you, holy Father!

We remember those
whose loved ones have died,
and all those who have finished
with earthly celebrations.
May they celebrate with you
and all the angels of heaven.

Silence

On this Christmas Day we want to say:
Thank you, holy Father!

For all the many blessings of this past year
and for all the good that you have enabled us to do;
for the experiences that have taught us
humility and patience,
we thank you.

Silence

On this Christmas Day we want to say:
Thank you, holy Father!

Merciful Father,
**accept these prayers
for the sake of your Son,
our Saviour Jesus Christ. Amen.**

Palm Sunday

*They took branches of palm trees and went
out to meet him, shouting 'Hosanna!'*
John 12:13

As we recall Jesus entering Jerusalem,
let us gather our thoughts to pray.

Father, as the crowds welcomed Jesus
and sang your praises,
we pray that many more will welcome you
into their hearts and lives over the coming year.
We pray for opportunities to spread your good news
and courage to take them.

Silence

You are our God:
we welcome you!

Father, we recall the donkey Jesus rode on,
and we pray for that real humility in our hearts
which treats status and image casually,
and truth and loving service seriously.

Silence

You are our God:
we welcome you!

Father, the children sang and shouted your praise,
and we pray for the children in homes,
throughout the land.
May we not fail them
in the support and teaching they need.

Silence

You are our God:
we welcome you!

Father, the crowds were responding
to the healing love they had seen in action in Jesus.
We bring to you in our love and imaginations now
all those we would have brought to Jesus
for healing and help.
Give them comfort and reassurance,
wholeness and hope.

Silence

You are our God:
we welcome you!

Father, Jesus knew he was riding to his death.
We pray for all on that last journey,
especially those burdened with fear and guilt.
We commend to your eternal love all who have died,
thanking you for the blessings we have received,
and even for the grief
which is part of the love we share.

Silence

You are our God:
we welcome you!

Father, we, too, spread our coats on the road
as we express our thankfulness
for all you have done for us
and the amazing extent of your love.

Merciful Father,
accept these prayers
for the sake of your Son,
our Saviour Jesus Christ. Amen.

Good Friday

He humbled himself and became obedient
to the point of death – even death on a cross.
Philippians 2:8

As we recall the extent of God's love for us,
let us pray.

Loving God, if we as the Church
are truly to be the body of Christ,
then let us stand at the foot of the cross
and learn what it means to love and keep on loving;
to serve and keep on serving.

Silence

Lord, in the light of the cross:
show us how to live.

If the world is ever to see real hope,
then purify and transform our lives
and stretch out our arms in loving forgiveness,
with no exceptions and no small print,
so that we shine as lights in the darkness.

Silence

Lord, in the light of the cross:
show us how to live.

If our work places and neighbourhoods and homes
are to display and respond to your values,
then make us more fervent in prayer,
more courageous in self-discipline
and, above all, more loving in outreach.

Silence

Lord, in the light of the cross:
show us how to live.

If the terrible suffering of extreme poverty,
injustice and oppression is to be addressed realistically,
then take away our greed and complacency
and our assumptions about appropriate living standards,
and teach us sacrificial self-giving
of time, energy and resources.

Silence

Lord, in the light of the cross:
show us how to live.

Father, through the life-giving death of Jesus,
may the dying turn to you
and know your merciful love;
may the grieving be comforted,
and may we all one day share
with those who have died
the eternal joy of your heaven.

Silence

Lord, in the light of the cross:
show us how to live.

Father, such amazing love is hard to grasp
and impossible to repay.
In thankfulness for lives set free to live
we offer you ourselves.

Merciful Father,
**accept these prayers
for the sake of your Son,
our Saviour Jesus Christ. Amen.**

Easter Day

*I am the resurrection and the life. Those who believe
in me, even though they die, will live.*
John 11:25

As we celebrate the new life of Resurrection,
let us pray to the one true God, who brings us all to life.

Lord God, we pray that the Church
may proclaim with joy your message of hope
for the world;
may our lives, as well as our worship,
testify to the truth of the Resurrection;
broaden our vision of what is possible
through new life in you.

Silence   Life-giving God:
                      transform our lives.

Lord God, we pray for the world we inhabit;
for those who lead, and take important decisions,
and for those who follow or are coerced,
or who have no voice.
We pray for mercy and justice, compassion and integrity.
We pray for protection against evil
and strengthening of goodness.

Silence   Life-giving God:
                      transform our lives.

Lord God, we pray for all babies, and those as yet unborn,
that they may be born into a world of love and acceptance.
We pray, too, for those who provide foster care,
and for all children at risk.

We pray for all parents and those who support them.
We pray for the newly baptised and recently confirmed;
for a deeper commitment to supporting one another
as we grow in faith.

Silence   Life-giving God:
                   transform our lives.

Lord God, we pray for those who cannot think,
for the pain or anguish which engulfs them;
for all whose lives are troubled and insecure;
for those who have little energy left to rejoice.
Bring healing, and the resources to cope with suffering,
and give us the grace
to carry one another's burdens in love.

Silence   Life-giving God:
                   transform our lives.

Lord God, we thank you for lives well lived,
and commend to your keeping those who have died.
Through the resurrection hope,
may they know the joy of heaven.

Silence   Life-giving God:
                   transform our lives.

Lord God, we thank you for the precious gift of new life;
may we never again take it for granted,
but live each moment in the fullness of life
that Jesus has gained for us.

Merciful Father,
**accept these prayers
for the sake of your Son,
our Saviour Jesus Christ. Amen.**

Pentecost

I will pour out my spirit on all flesh.
Joel 2:28

As the body of Christ,
in the power of the Spirit,
let us pray.

For a fresh outpouring of the Holy Spirit
on the people of God all over the world,
and in all worship traditions.
For a readiness to be changed and made new;
for a softening of the ground of our hearts
to receive without fear.

Silence

With our whole selves we pray:
come, Holy Spirit of God.

For all the peoples of the earth
to know you and honour your name.
For the healing of the nations
and a new thirst for righteousness and purity
at every level and in every aspect of society.
For a dissatisfaction with the pursuit of pleasure
and all that distracts us from our true calling.

Silence

With our whole selves we pray:
come, Holy Spirit of God.

For the grace and power to live out our faith
in the real and challenging world,
among those we meet and eat with,

whose lives we share,
without compromising that calling
to be the body of Christ,
living God's integrity and purity,
forgiveness and love.

Silence

With our whole selves we pray:
come, Holy Spirit of God.

For those whose lives feel empty or cheated,
or filled with pain, or worry or guilt.
For all whose hopes and dreams are in tatters;
all who are in any way imprisoned.

Silence

With our whole selves we pray:
come, Holy Spirit of God.

For those who walk the dark journey of death
and all who have come through it
into your presence;
for mourners distressed by regrets
or angry with God at their loss.

Silence

With our whole selves we pray:
come, Holy Spirit of God.

For all you have in store for us, we thank you;
we look forward to walking into the future
of your promise, alive with your life.

Merciful Father,
accept these prayers
for the sake of your Son,
our Saviour Jesus Christ. Amen.

INDEXES

Topical Index

N.B. Each set of prayers includes intercessions for the dying or those who have died.

Biblical Index